MW00848630

NIGHT VISION

✿

NIGHT VISION

✿

CLAIRE
WAHMANHOLM

NEW MICHIGAN PRESS
TUCSON, ARIZONA

NEW MICHIGAN PRESS

DEPT OF ENGLISH, P. O. BOX 210067

UNIVERSITY OF ARIZONA

TUCSON, AZ 85721-0067

<http://newmichiganpress.com>

Orders and queries to <nmp@thediagram.com>.

ISBN 978-1-934832-62-2. FIRST PRINTING.

Printed in the United States of America.

Design by Ander Monson.

Cover art by Daniel Lupton.

CONTENTS

BEGINNING

A pulling began from nowhere. Book bindings came unglued, hairline cracks cobwebbed the backs of our hands. Caught in the middle of this force we could not call by name, we waited. Down by the river, no more boats. Even the docks had been uprooted and stacked on the shore. For a long time we tried not to move, tried to feel in the air where the pulling was coming from. Groups of us stood with our index fingers licked and raised. How long did we stand before we put our hands to our chests? Irregular thumps. Just there, just here. Kaleidoscope of wrong rhythms. Looking at the night sky, we could see new patches of darkness coming alive. Mornings were suddenly birdless, cloudless, without wind, bright deserts. Now we began to wonder whether we had done wrong things. Or rather, we began to wonder which of our wrong things had been wrong enough. Putting our hands out in the dark of our basements, we felt gaps in the limestone where there had been none. Quarries filled with unidentifiable slurry overnight. Rotten fish slapped their rotten smell on the riverbank. Something was going to happen, had already begun happening, but no one wanted to be here when it finished. There was one way out of the city. Under the streets was a set of sewers that led to the sea. Very carefully, we lowered ourselves into their metal mouths, leaving all the lights on in our houses. Whatever was watching us might be fooled. Xenon lamps shone like suns from the sewer walls, burning our skin. Yarn unspooled behind us as we walked deeper and deeper in. Zero—as in *ground,* as in *vanishing point,* as in *where the reckoning begins.*

we

had

a taste for

error

and

frail

boats

.   o   ye

brave

sailors   in

an

unexplored

sky.

we

strayed from home

and

failed utterly

on

the shores of space

THE JELLYFISH

We emerged like cicadas from under the catastrophe. We stood on the beach and watched meteoroids plink into the sea. The purple sky was clear. All the jellyfish had washed ashore and sat in plump, dense circles on the sand. Someone prodded one with a stick. We could see through its crystal cap. Its indigo bell bent the sand beneath it at an angle. Was a thick pulp tremor. The purple sky was clear. We could see inside the jellyfish body. We could see the brick dust and the oil and the teeth lodged in the mesoglea alongside the gonads and the gut and the mouth. We gingerly bagged the jellyfish as evidence. We could see the poison pulsing through its glass noodle tentacles. We too felt seen through by something. We covered our eyes with our hands until the purple light pulsed through them like stained glass.

MISERY RIFT

Plate tectonics had accelerated. Deep lakes appeared overnight, acres and acres of water pasture. It started in the Great Rift Valley and spread like a prairie fire. We called it the *Misery Rift*, and in its generous speed, the land unpinched itself so quickly that our loved ones' waving hands faded like sails. We thought that if we stood perfectly still for some time, we would someday feel their warm backs meet ours in a new Pangaea of skin. So we stood, our raised arms hardening into stone, our handkerchiefs slowly shredding in the wind. Crows harvested beard lichen from our mouths and replaced it with their husky calls. Songbirds laid eggs in the dips of our clavicles and in the pits of our upturned hands. We had thought the Earth was finite, that it was only a matter of time before everything returned to its origin. But the lost ones never reappeared at our backs. We couldn't stand forever. Land was ebbing even faster than anyone thought it would. Every morning there was a new, farther stretch of blue.

The ocean calls.

we

cross   six

trillion miles of

everlasting night.

we

are precious

tendrils of light.

We

may be a

sun to someone.

Why should we

be

utterly lost

STILL THE SEA

No dilution. The hole in us grew and grew. We had hoped that time might shovel its dirt into our wells and rifts, might fill up our grief-spaces, but it just kept flinging spades of air into our faces. We couldn't stand the way our hearts staggered around in our chests, tumbling east and west and forgetting where the past was. We started eating soil to keep them in place. We swallowed pebbles. Our hearts did not settle, but thumped more wildly, sought stones to bruise themselves on. We forced larger and larger rocks down, ate more and more mud, but still the sea inside us was empty and sharp, the blue water we had turned away from large and greedy at our backs.

NO STARS

We walked inland. We entered a ruined schoolhouse and stood before the board's blank sea. No waves. No white. We thought to make a timeline but had already forgotten the beginning. I looked out the empty window at the purple light. No stars. When had that happened? And where was the light coming from? I drew a year that was a white boat on a green sea. I whitened the water with waving arms, then smudged them out. We would drown out here. I could already feel the weight of less and less air. I pressed my palm to the board and felt it shudder. We all pressed our palms to the board and left black five-pointed stars that cast no light. Outside, the year went by. Our stars turned beneath the purple sky.

THE PIT

We almost fell into it. We were walking with our noses so low to the ground that we didn't notice the ground was ending. But suddenly darkness. Suddenly space and near weightlessness. We dug in our heels and sat back before it, looked down into its planet-sized mouth. We shaped our mouths to the shape of the pit-mouth, yawned so wide we thought we would split. We built a set of huts next to it, daubed their walls with our muddy handprints. We lit fires and killed wild animals and carved their bones into cudgels, sharpened our eyes until they could wound. From raptors we pulled feathers the length of our arms. When bored, we played augur with our piles of bones, gripped our own thumbs like lucky rabbits' feet, like tiny warm grenades. At night we stood on the cliffs and looked as deep as we could into the eye of the pit and sometimes thought we saw a pupil of light. What was so bright that it shone up to us at this height? At night we lay with our eyes glazed but open, squeezing our rabbits' feet until they turned white.

We grow up

        frozen
      like

icy moons

  .

    our brothers and sisters

Are

giant snow-balls   .
Every now and then
    the ice is vaporized

by

an inferno of
    light.

RELAXATION TAPE

We listened to relaxation tapes to help us sleep. The purple sky was too bright and all our pillows were made of rawhide, so night after night we lay on our cots while a woman's voice cooed at us over the loudspeakers. We found a comfortable position. We let our legs, then arms, then neck go limp. We knew the script by heart. We would walk down a forest path dappled with light. The sun would feel just right on our faces. The air would be cool but comfortable. We would not panic. *Clench your fists,* said the voice. I clenched my fists. *Focus on where it hurts,* it said. I did. Then I relaxed and let the tension float away like smoke on the wind. Beneath my feet was soft moss. Beneath my palms was bark. *Remember that you can return to this place whenever you'd like.* We remembered. We felt very comfortable and at ease. We were climbing a gentle hill made of tires. The ground was dappled with bleach. We felt a light breeze. *A scenic lookout awaits you at the top of the hill.* Our bodies were becoming very warm and very heavy. We felt very comfortable and at ease. Bodies were dropping from the trees. *Continue to enjoy this peaceful place. Continue to breathe.*

THE FACTORY

Grubby violet dusk. Everywhere, the tongue-tang of rust. Everywhere endless grass. We pushed the truck until it stopped beside a huge rhizome of concrete and broken glass. We pulled our faces out of its violet shards and stared into the dark mass of the factory's throat. In buildings like this, some of us had bottled glue, stitched animal skin coats. We remembered sweet blood in the hinges of our hands, fur in our lungs. Now we clambered over the toothless windowsills and landed on the factory's cool concrete tongue. Rooms of animal suits, rooms of hooves, of hoses. Dark drains. One by one the others put on their palomino coats. Then were gone, their long legs leaving a wound in my throat. Outside, the prairie was empty and hot. Beneath my palm the prairie's heaving slowed to a trot, to a walk. Beneath my palm the prairie rolled over and stopped.

RELAXATION TAPE

Nightmares were spreading like oil on water, but there was a tape for that too. As we lay on our rawhide cots, the woman's voice asked us to *imagine a scary situation we couldn't escape from.* We imagined quicksand. We imagined being handcuffed and pushed out of an airplane. We imagined being blinded and locked in a burning house. *Now imagine,* sang the loudspeaker, *that you have grown a pair of wings.* We imagined. *You are flying up and up, away from the nightmare, away from the danger.* We flew. We looked down on our fear. *It feels wonderful to fly,* soothed the voice. We closed our eyes and saw a man soaring ahead of us in the sky. His wings were fuchsia curtains on his back. His wings were fuchsia skin that flaked and feathered as he flew away from his burning house. We caught the ash on our tongues but we were *completely safe now,* we knew that nothing could reach us way up here. We breathed in lungfuls of cloud whose droplets felt nothing like sand grains in our mouths. The airplanes from which we were falling were nothing but our own bird-shapes hurtling over the ground.

ALMANAC

We had grown leaky. Our heads were full of fissures that wouldn't seal no matter how tightly we clamped the jaws of the vise around our temples. Our scalps wept until only the present rattled in our ears, bone dry and rabid. We walked around the corner or we had been walking for years. We entered the same empty house at the end of the same dirt road. In every room I found a yellow almanac under the bed and read the same page, which told me the time that Neptune would rise in the sky, which told me the time that civil dusk would descend. I pressed the almanac to my head. What was *time?* What was *descend?* Every time I left the house I took the almanac with me. I slept with it under my rawhide pillow, hoping that while I slept, my head would somehow mend. Every night I dreamed of frost spreading across a ragged field, knitting the furrows with its uniform white.

in

a dank and forgotten   library
consecrated to   mold   .

The scholars of the library studied

and

mapped

us,

compiled   the
dead   .

in

ten large

dissecting rooms

,

we   were

disintegrated,

pathetic scattered fragments.
there was on the library shelves a book.
the tragedy of

our

wonder   was in it.

FUSE

One morning we woke with bombs in our bellies. We could feel the sutures there, and there—their raised, tender red. We knew they were bombs because of the way they ticked. Like a pulse, but not in line with our pulses. Like an enormous cricket, but we could tell it wasn't alive. Our bellies stayed cold and heavy. When we walked, our feet sank deep in the mud. When we tried to climb trees, the branches broke with a crack, with a tick. We learned to land gently. No one knew where the bombs came from. No one knew how to defuse them or what might set them off. We stayed calm, made breezy motions, breathed in through our noses and out through our mouths. When the wind blew, we bent with it. When the river dragged us downstream, we let it, tried to make ourselves small and soft around the rocks. After many months, someone finally thought to cut the danger out. We watched her press her knife to the sutures, watched the knife enter the sutures and come back empty. Nothing to remove. Nothing to prove there had ever been a bomb. Nothing that even bled. Only the soft body, only the red.

in   a flash of light,

        I   made myself

a   road

                ,

    an   Earth   of

            atoms

                    ,

no   limit

        ,

        no

            future

RELAXATION TAPE

We were asked to start with our eyes open. The loudspeaker asked us to imagine that we were made of jelly. It told us to let our bones be moss, to let them melt like salt into the mud. We looked skyward and the loudspeaker became a prayer. *Let your lips uncouple, your jaws dissolve; let your mouth fall open.* We did. We opened our mouths onto the dark, opened them toward the surrounding woods. *And now imagine that your bones are leaves.* I saw the melted trees, the acid-rained twigs. Through my open mouth I drew night air. *And now imagine that your mouth is soil.* I shut my eyes and imagined letting them sink from their sockets, letting them sink through my skull to leave two open eyes blacking the back of my head. I took what used to be my hand and let it rest on what used to be my stomach. *Imagine you are nothing.* I did not have to imagine. The membranes over my organs had melted. I was half buried in the soft mud. *Let go*, a voice said. I did. I opened earthward. Afterward, stories would imagine this melting as the emptying of us, but no emptiness could have left us so open.

BEASTS

I was the first one to see them. For many nights, the others had been describing a strange scent. A new one, not our own. We all knew the particular timbre of our combined smell. Now there was an unease, an out-of-tuning that cast strange shadows on the path and raised thick forests where there had been none. One black afternoon, among these new trees, I counted our eyes, the sheen of the fire upon them. Far too many. Far too close. When daylight flickered on again I lost them in my tender blinking. I took out my eyes so they could not lie. I cut off my ears so they could not mishear. Still I knew the beasts were there, the sulfur of their fur thick on my tongue, their musk thick in the roots of my hair. I could still smell the others on the air, but farther and farther, more and more air between us. More and more sulfur. More and more fur.

THE CARRION FLOWER

In the forest we found a small red well, an empty pupil, a bucket with petals. Some of us could fit our entire hands inside of it. Some of us could fit our heads. We spread our arms to haul it from the ground. It seemed to weigh the weight of a child, though none of us had seen one in a while. *They looked like us,* said someone, *only small. Like dolls,* said someone else. We all remembered the weight of them on our laps, our knees. We remembered building them houses in the trees, balancing their soft mass above us as we lay on the leaves. But no one could conjure the pitch of their voices or the shape of their cheeks. And we found that no one wanted to let the flower go, so we took turns hefting it up and down the forest's uneven aisles. Some of us bore it better than others. Some of us didn't even gag at the body bag smell. I for one held no perfumed rag to my nose, dreamt of no sweet roses. When the flies arrived I opened my mouth as wide as it would go.

THE KITTENS

The jellyfish was starting to stink. Its fragrant weight unspooled behind us like a loose bobbin. Its pulp blurred our footprints as we dragged it across the dust desert. The bag was heavy with it. We couldn't drag it forever. I thought of the gunnysack kittens of our childhood that we were told wouldn't survive. I thought of ourselves, long dead without knowing it, only just now knowing it, looking around suddenly realizing we weren't breathing. How was the dust still here? How could we think about the kittens? We were dragging ourselves behind us through the desert. There wasn't enough time. The thought of kittens was 98% water and rapidly evaporating. Beneath each grain of sand was an anti-grain. Beneath each memory of the kittens was an anti-kitten, an anti-memory, a shadow-shape that darkened the desert. Our mouths were full of hazard. We pulled at the gunnysack with our fingers. Did we also meowl to be born into the black water?

men   wander

           among

                                   us   ,
           fierce

           ,   a great
many   .

      We are surrounded

      by
Ten thousand   large
                animals   who

      hunt in packs
                    . Our
generations

                         become
                 extinct.

BOG BODY

Our torsos were swamps we swam in. All the time
surrounded by bog and sphagnum. We knew we would
become carbon sinks, but just now we had to keep moving,
keep our bog bodies afloat. We thought that maybe time
would repair us, but here we were paddling with one
wrist loose, a kneecap gone missing. Somewhere, space
was collecting all these lost things. We imagined that
space as a bog through which they would sink and be
held, pickled, in tannic water. That was one of our better
thoughts. It helped us live longer. When we found safe
places we stopped and buried our faces in the ditches of
our hands, deep in their dirt. Water wept through our
finger-reeds, seeped through the sedge. While we slept
we ran hedge mazes to try to separate ourselves from
our peaty, sulfur smell. We had terrible dreams where
everything we'd ever lost was returned to us. Some woke
with tears in their ears. Some refused to wake at all. Every
day someone would sit down in the forest and wait to be
eaten by moss. The forest had never been so soft.

REAP

With our heads loose and wobbling, we did strange
things. Someone climbed to the top of a tower and flew
off. Someone chewed through a pound of shredded
cans. I stuck both my hands inside a rattlesnake den
and clapped until my arms broke off at the elbow. They
thrashed rustedly at my feet, filling the clouds with
creaking. In a nearby field I found a body with all its parts
still intact and dragged it back to the factory. I passed
someone filling their boots with snow. I passed someone
burning a pile of their own hair. On their bare head I
could see the bolts, the blue maps someone had drawn
in crayon: *dig here* and *don't dig here*. I could see the
head tilting on its axis, the hair-smoke scudding around
it. I continued dragging my body toward the factory. I
attached my new arms as best I could. Everything I held
was a little crooked. My face wobbled like an unshelled
egg. When I reached down to touch the earth it shied
away and fled.

RELAXATION TAPE

Some of us didn't have lungs left. So when we lay beneath the loudspeaker sky—when we were told to *pay attention to our breath*, we had to improvise. Last week at the burn pit I'd found a concertina and hooked it to my chest. Now, when I *inhaled to the count of three*, I pulled apart its honeycomb bellows and felt myself fill. I pushed them together and the air moved through my mouth like wind through a dead canyon. The bellows inhaled again. I remembered the rhythm of breathing, the ease of it, the mindless fall and rise, the non-travail. *And now exhale*, the static sang. *And now imagine a billowing sail*. I saw the waves behind my eyes, the bobbing boat. *And now count back from five*. The ocean swelled. *And now from four*. The ocean burned with oil. *From three*. I opened my eyes. Everyone pumped their squeezeboxes. The breeze of it flushed vultures from the trees.

at the end   , we   turn   blue
        beyond   imagining .

     we are in   pain   no

soft meadows

       here   , but
our search for them
          is

  long

         ,

longest
          at the
bottom of a deep well

we

        cast no shadow

THE LAST ANIMALS

We saw them from the top of the hill. The wind blew past our ears and down into the valley where they straggled, up to their tails in snow. One spotted, one striped, one the color of dead leaves. Our encyclopedia had told us about animals, but none of us had ever seen a real one. To see the last of something wasn't new. We had seen many last things: the last acorn, the last lightning storm, the last tide. All the last things had the same smell—a solvent, a sulfur we could taste on the air—which is how we always knew to pay attention. The animals were moving steadily across the valley. We passed around the encyclopedia and studied the pictures, but none of them matched. Someone broke a stick from the last tree and tried to scratch the animals' outlines into the frozen dirt of the last vegetable patch, but it wouldn't take. The animals were crossing the valley faster than we could follow. Our nails broke as we raked at the soil. When we next looked up, our eyes filled with snow.

the   dark

is everywhere

is

a confusion   , We

are profoundly

lonely   a   reed

In the

Sea

.

NIGHT VISION

The Earth turned more slowly now. Nights were days long and days were overcast with coal. So much darkness made our eyes bulge like plums, made them burn like fireballs. We became very swift. We became very deft hunters. We could see very deeply into each other, all the way to the marrow. When one of us stood against the moon, the others could watch her blood rush through her like a river. We could see the air bubbles where the stomach and heart should be. And if we didn't blink we could watch them shrink. And if we didn't breathe we could feel our own cells tightening into pebbles. And if we wanted, we could scoop handfuls of ourselves into the well we stood at the bottom of and thereby build ourselves a stairway out. And once out would face the sky with our meteorite eyes. Would see all the way to the end of it for the first time.

the world is very   distant   . We

know   the

                                  humdrum

                    immensity of space

          . We   know that our universe

                              is

          merely a

                                        glimpse

                                   of   the

          end

THE LODESTARS

The grief did not bear down on us, nor did the panic, nor the despair. Rather they rose up the wells of our bodies like mercury. If we stood still for too long, our heels softened into sponges and we drew these things up into us from the mud or the tarmac. Sometimes we dangled our feet in the ocean to feel the alarm of salt seep into our skin. Sometimes we woke to find the tide of it had risen while we slept and the terror had collared our necks. We ached for the jellyfish we had drug inland, picturing its nerve net pulsing immortally through that water. Most of us only stood still in shifts, but some planted themselves like sign posts, like lodestars. Sometimes we passed their balefire bodies on the highways. The scarecrow eyes that burned a fever in our own. The stiff spread arms that marked a path of no return. From our watchtowers we stood and narrated their patterns into new myths we had always known. Once upon a time the soil raised a blade to our throats. Once upon a time the sun wiped its bloody hand across us while we slept.

NOTES

The erasures are all taken from Carl Sagan's *Cosmos* (1980).

ACKNOWLEDGMENTS

Grateful acknowledgment is made to the editors of the following journals where these poems, sometimes in earlier versions and under different titles, first appeared:

"Fuse," *Anthropoid*
"Beginning," "The Jellyfish," "Misery Rift,"
    DIAGRAM
"Relaxation Tape," *Elsewhere*
"No Stars," "Almanac," *Fog Machine*
"The Last Animals," *Glass: A Journal of Poetry*
"The Lodestars," *Handsome*
"Bog Body," "The Pit," *Newfound*
"Relaxation Tape," "Relaxation Tape," *PANK*
"Beasts," "Night Vision," "Reap," *Paperbag*
"[In a Dank and Forgotten Library]," "[The Ocean
    Calls]," "[The World is Very Distant]," "[We
    Grow Up Frozen]," "[We Had a Taste for Error],"
    Saltfront
"Relaxation Tape," "The Factory," *TXTOBJX*
"The Carrion Flower," *Winter Tangerine*

CLAIRE WAHMANHOLM holds degrees from UW-Madison, the Writing Seminars at the Johns Hopkins University, and the University of Utah. Her poems have appeared in, or are forthcoming from, *Saltfront, PANK, Paperbag, Anthropoid, Bennington Review, Bateau, DIAGRAM, Best New Poets 2015, Memorious, Handsome, The Journal, The Kenyon Review Online,* and *32 Poems*. Her debut full-length collection is forthcoming from Tinderbox Editions in early 2019. She lives and teaches in the Twin Cities.

❁

COLOPHON

Text is set in a digital version of Jenson, designed by Robert Slimbach in 1996, and based on the work of punchcutter, printer, and publisher Nicolas Jenson. The titles here are in Futura.

✺

NEW MICHIGAN PRESS, based in Tucson, Arizona,
prints poetry and prose chapbooks, especially work that
transcends traditional genre. Together with DIAGRAM,
NMP sponsors a yearly chapbook competition.

DIAGRAM, a journal of text, art, and schematic, is
published bimonthly at THEDIAGRAM.COM. Periodic
print anthologies are available from the New Michigan
Press at NEWMICHIGANPRESS.COM.

CPSIA information can be obtained
at www.ICGtesting.com
Printed in the USA
FFOW03n1641130218
45072511-45466FF

9 781934 832622